Must-read for any political, community, or business leader. The process outlined here will ensure effective engagement of your broader community. If followed, it will save you a lot of heartache.

—David E. Woods, mayor and council member, East Palo Alto

The authors pack more than twenty years of experience as facilitators and as leadership-effectiveness experts into The Moment of Oh!, *an easy-to-read and thoughtful guide for citizens and others who are motivated to do what's right for their communities. They clearly articulate the "stages" inherent in just about every community issue—and then help the reader navigate it all to a successful outcome.*

—Lance Robertson, public-affairs manager, Eugene Water & Electric Board

Greg and John have outlined a community-engagement process that really works. I only wish this book had been available in my early days as a city councilman; it would have saved me hours of learning how to effectively engage my residents and provided a much-needed framework for healthy community decision making.

—Pete Constant, San José city-council member, District 1

The Moment of Oh! *offers a wonderful framework for civic leaders as they work to guide their communities through tough decision-making processes. It is versatile and adaptable to communities of any size and to decisions of all kinds. Civic leaders from elected officials to city managers owe it to themselves to investigate* The Moment of Oh!

—John Oberst, mayor of Monmouth, Oregon

The Moment of *Oh!*

Making Community Decisions

A Guide for Community Leaders and Public Officials

Highlighting Five Stages and Seven Core Principles
for Robust and Widely Supported Community Decisions

by John Blakinger & Greg Ranstrom
Illustrations by Concepts Captured™

A CIVILSAY™ Publication
©2012
http://www.civilsay.net

Contents

*The strength of free peoples resides
in the local community.*

— Alexis de Tocqueville
Democracy in America
1835

Introduction

Public servants and community leaders get a lot of things right. Because of their efforts, their communities enjoy services and benefits that the community rarely needs to consider. However, a few crucial decisions can become lightning rods for communities we know. This guide was written with those high-voltage community decisions in mind.

We, the authors, sit on local public committees, and we design community-engagement processes. Through our experience we know that even the most contentious issues can be resolved for the good of the community and that each decision process can strengthen the community's capacity to solve subsequent challenges.

We have spent many hours dissecting the essential elements of tough community-decision processes. We each used one current project as a reference to ensure our insights were grounded in real-world application. Greg referenced his work with a network of ninety organizations attempting to shift the dynamics of prosperity and poverty in Santa Clara County, California. John referenced his work with a contentious groundwater-contamination issue in Deschutes and Klamath County, Oregon.

Through a series of long conversations and the collaborative writing process, we have been able to articulate our framework for solving tough community problems. Our approach starts from the perspective of the individual community member and considers his or her current level of engagement with the issue.

This guide is for community leaders and public officials who genuinely believe in open and democratic public processes. It is written for those who intend to act with integrity and in the best interests of their communities. In our experience most leaders fall into that category.

In the first part of the book, we identify and describe the five stages of engagement. These stages help the leader understand the trajectory of the community's decision-making process and determine the best steps to ensure the process goes as well as possible. They are easy to remember, but they take discipline to apply:

- *What? (unaware of issue)*
- *No! (resistant to change)*
- *Oh! (urge to act)*
- *Whoa! (overwhelmed by complexity)*
- *Let's Go! (energized by the decision)*

We emphasize the Moment of *Oh!* because people understand exactly what we are talking about when we describe that distinct point in time when a person or group discovers that action is required to either avoid negative consequences or to seize an opportunity. We believe that the Moment of *Oh!* is at the center of misunderstandings in community decision making, because once someone has reached the Moment of *Oh!*, they are inclined to want to move forward, rather than help others reach their own Moment of *Oh!*. When community leaders impatiently move forward, groups of citizens get left behind, and the process stumbles or fails. When leaders help community members through the stages of engagement, the decision process works.

The second part of the book identifies seven core principles that must be present for healthy community decision making.

The principles also become a guide for distinct actions leaders can take to help move a community to a positive solution. We didn't create the principles and then try to apply them; rather, we looked at processes in which we were directly involved and teased out the essential principles that guided our actions. These are the principles we live by.

- *Include Diverse Perspectives*
- *Understand Each Other*
- *Use Experts Wisely*
- *Expect It to be Messy*
- *Make Decisions on Shared Facts*
- *Take One Step at a Time*
- *Leave Tracks*

We wrote this guide out of our deep respect for leaders who are willing to bring together communities around tough challenges. We hope we can make your job a little easier and a lot more fulfilling as you guide community decisions and build an ever-stronger foundation of trust and respect wherever you serve.

The Five Stages of Engagement

Each individual experiences a progression of reactions or stages when confronted with a problem or an opportunity. These stages gauge the level of commitment the person has toward resolving the problem or capitalizing on the opportunity (see figure).

The What? Stage

On first contact with a problem, a person often responds with, "What are you talking about?"

"What makes this problem more important than all the other things I have to deal with?"

"What does this issue mean to me?"

An individual in the *What?* stage does not understand or accept the problem.

The No! Stage

As a person is exposed to more information about the issue, disinterest shifts to various strategies of resistance.

"No, I never use that government service. Why would I care where the building is? And I have to mow the lawn right now anyway."

"No. Why do I care where my water comes from? I have important things to deal with; the school just called, and my son is in trouble again."

This initial resistance can be overcome when the individual sees his or her own interests as closely aligned with the consequences of the problem or the possible outcomes of the opportunity.

The Oh! Stage (or the Moment of *Oh!*)

As an individual gathers more information and achieves an understanding of the consequences of the problem, there is a realization that something *must* be done. This is the Moment of *Oh!*

"Oh! You mean folks are going to drive right by my house? How many cars a day will that be?"

"My water rate is going up 50 percent? That has to be a mistake!"

The Whoa! Stage

After experiencing the Moment of *Oh!*, individuals want to find a solution. Oftentimes the solution requires accepting some negative consequences. Then people experience the stage of *Whoa!*

"*Whoa!* If the office isn't moved, my taxes are going up?"

"I need water for fire protection, and clean water is essential, but there has to be a cheaper solution."

The Let's Go! Stage

Once people assess the pros and cons of the solution and make their decision, the response is *Let's Go!* Communities that manage to engage people through each stage of engagement will be able to implement community decisions more effectively. Community members will regard public officials and community leaders as responsive stewards of the community's best interests.

Assessment of which stage of engagement community members are experiencing is critical to designing strategies to arrive at widely supported community decisions. Next we will examine each stage of engagement in more detail.

Leading with the Five Stages of Engagement

Getting to the Moment of Oh! and ultimately, Let's Go!

While it would be much easier if all community members reached the Moment of *Oh!* simultaneously, the reality is that each person travels through the five stages of engagement at his or her own pace. In addition the needs of individuals change as they move through the stages. Community leaders must allow for these various needs. In this section we will describe how to recognize an individual's stage of engagement, how the individual can impact other community members, and what can be done to satisfy the individual's needs so he or she can move to the next stage of engagement.

We wrote this book especially for those high-voltage situations that require an extraordinary degree of community engagement, regardless of the ultimate authority for the final decision. When facing a tough issue, community leaders must clearly communicate how the decision will be made and who has the decision authority. Community leaders must garner community acceptance of the ultimate decision—regardless of the "official" process. We have seen too many decisions derail even when the decision process followed every rule and law. Paying attention to the stages of engagement helps ensure that quality decisions are ultimately implemented for the public good.

Stage 1: What?

A person in the *What?* stage of the commitment curve lacks relevant factual information. He or she either knows nothing about the situation or may have misunderstandings about the facts and their relevance to the situation.

For the person who lacks information, the leader must provide the facts—starting with the basic, foundational information—and build from there. A person lacking information becomes more informed when the leader can connect the situation to information the person already understands.

For a person with misinformation, the leader must understand what the person believes. Sometimes what seems like misinformation to the leader is actually a perspective the leader has not considered. For example, a community member might know something about federal environmental standards that is relevant to the community decision. The leader must not casually toss this "misinformation" aside. Look instead for ways to learn what has led to the person's position and what part of the information may be based on relevant facts.

The leader should not argue about which facts are relevant. Arguing often causes the person to cling more tightly to what he or she believes. It will take time for a person to unlearn misunderstandings and replace them with a relevant, fact-based perspective.

At this stage the leader should focus on understanding the individual's perspective and begin to establish a set of community-relevant, shared facts about the situation.

Characteristics of a person in the What? stage:

- *uninformed*
- *misinformed*

What the person needs to proceed to the next stage:

- *the relevant facts*
- *chance to assimilate new facts and let go of irrelevant and inaccurate information*

How the leader can help:

- *Gather and elicit relevant facts and provide them to the community.*
- *Provide opportunities to have conversations about each other's facts.*
- *Listen for and incorporate new, relevant facts.*

Stage 2: No!

No! is a natural response for most people when they are confronted with a situation that may require a response. Resistance to change should be an expected and accepted part of any community-decision process. Different people will spend varying amounts of time in the *No!* stage. Sometimes it just takes time for the reality of the situation to sink in. In some cases people will move back into the *What?* stage to check on their understanding of the issue. During the *No!* stage, the focus should be on continuing to provide more information and, importantly, providing time for individuals to unpack and repack their thoughts through conversation.

No! can also help clarify exactly what is at stake for various individuals and groups. The *No!* stage is very helpful for community leaders to learn how an issue impacts community members and what parts of the issue are of greater or lesser importance to which groups. Leaders should welcome the *No!* stage as an opportunity to gain more clarity around the issue and its effect on community members. Leaders can prepare themselves for the *No!* stage by articulating the issue as clearly as possible and asking the following question: When and/or how will people feel the impact of the decisions we make?

Complex community-decision processes will attract some dissenters who will remain in the *No!* stage throughout the process. The dissenters' motives might be well meaning, but they could also be vindictive, ideological, political, or simply self-serving. Community members may or may not disclose their motives. In all cases community leaders should continue to invite and listen to dissenting views. The art is to build a relationship with the dissenters even if their views are not adopted by the community. Dissenting opinions become a part of the community's reality. The dissent must be acknowledged, and the dissenters should be respected, especially as the community moves forward.

Both the *What?* and the *No!* stages are often characterized by community rumors, half-truths, and innuendo. In the absence of shared understanding, community members latch on to small bits of information, unfounded concerns, and improbable scenarios. Meetings can and will be sidetracked by community members who do not yet—and might never—agree with fundamental assumptions and shared facts.

Leaders must expend extra effort at this stage to ask questions of uninformed or dissenting community members to understand how they have arrived at their opinions. By asking questions the leader demonstrates respect and broadens the dialogue to allow for further education about the issue. Asking questions at this stage is not just about educating community members. Leaders are often surprised by what they learn about specific concerns and interests, which can be incorporated into the eventual solution.

Characteristics of a person in the No! stage:

- *disinterested*
- *focused on other things*
- *resistant*
- *avoidant*
- *negative*
- *dismissive*
- *already biased*
- *prejudiced about process*

What this person needs to proceed to the next stage:

- *He or she needs to connect the situation to his or her own interests and determine his or her specific concerns related to the issue.*

How the leader can help:

- *Anticipate others' concerns based upon their interests.*
- *Confront "no" with "I think this matters to you because...."*
- *Confront "no" with "Help me understand how you have come to this point of view."*

Stage 3: Oh!

The Moment of *Oh!* is the key stage where a person pivots from understanding the problem to a desire to *solve* the problem. The leader's action when a person reaches the Moment of *Oh!* varies depending on how many community members have arrived at the Moment of *Oh!*

When many members of the community, including those with diverse perspectives, have reached the Moment of *Oh!*, the community is ready to move to solution development. Beware, however, that many community members arriving at this stage at the same time is not the norm.

Typically there is a small but growing number of people who, once they reach the Moment of *Oh!*, have the desire and the need to act. The community can't, however, proceed to solution development until more people arrive at this stage.

A fundamental question that can help others arrive at the Moment of *Oh!* is this: "What will happen if we do nothing about this issue?" When the consequences of doing nothing are deemed unacceptable to an individual, he or she has arrived at the Moment of *Oh!*

The leader should first acknowledge an individual's Moment of *Oh!* and desire to act. Understanding the basis for the Moment of *Oh!* is valuable in getting other people to arrive as well. It is therefore useful to help the individual articulate how and why he or she arrived at the Moment of *Oh!* and to encourage him or her to help other community members follow the path to the Moment of *Oh!* We call this *leaving tracks*, which we describe in more detail later as one of the seven core principles.

Characteristics of a person in the Oh! stage:
- *impatient for action*
- *has a solution*
- *impatient with others who haven't "gotten it" yet*

What the person needs to proceed to the next stage:
- *a path to deciding on a solution*
- *something to do while waiting for others in the community to get to the Moment of **Oh!***

How the leader can help:
- *Affirm the person's Moment of **Oh!***
- *Ask the person how he or she would like to be involved in the solution.*
- *Help individuals describe their individual paths to the Moment of **Oh!** so others can follow.*
- *Ask individuals about the consequences of doing nothing.*

Stage 4: Whoa!

Once a sufficient percentage of community members with multiple perspectives and interests have reached the Moment of *Oh!*, the urge is to act immediately, to jump right to *Let's Go!* But as individuals begin to recognize the unanticipated impacts and costs of the solution, the tendency is to pull back from the urge to act. Leaders can help by continuing to remind people about their broad consensus around what needs to be addressed while not pushing too fast toward a single solution. This slowing down of the process is very useful for the community, allowing time for multiple possible solutions to be designed and vetted before choosing the best option.

Whoa! is also the stage when people who have not already become involved get very interested. They see that something is going to happen, investments will be made, and things will change. In a sense they have their own Moment of *Oh!*— "Oh, people are serious about doing something. I better get involved if I want to have a say in this!"

Because new people are attracted to the community conversation at this point, there is more reason for the leader to move forward deliberately, but slowly enough to bring people onboard with the process. It makes no sense to disregard people who haven't previously shown any interest. In fact the leader should welcome new participants as an indication that the process is moving forward and on track. The leader should expect late arrivals to the process and create easy access and paths for participation.

Whoa! is also the time to put extra effort into recruiting diverse participation. The integrity of the community solution will be at risk if important community players have not participated in the process. If open invitations to the process fail to attract needed participation, then personal outreach by community leaders may be necessary.

Characteristics of a person in the Whoa! stage:
- *overwhelmed by the reality of the situation*
- *annoyed by latecomers to the community-decision process*
- *impatient with the process (especially if a particular solution is favored)*

What a person needs to proceed to the next stage:
- *a clear timeline and process for deciding on a solution*
- *to see how their interests and concerns inform the possible solutions*
- *confirmation that the divergent solution possibilities will converge*
- *clear solution criteria*

How the leader can help:
- *Confirm the person's interests and concerns and how they connect to the possible solutions.*
- *Remind people of the messy, divergent solution-development process necessary to arrive at a sound solution.*
- *Continually remind people of the process and timelines.*
- *Help the community define criteria that will be used to assess the possible solutions.*

Stage 5: Let's Go!

Let's Go! may be the easiest stage of the process. If the community has followed the process and made a well-informed decision, then implementation has a much better chance to go smoothly.

Ongoing communication is still critical, and new community members may still become interested only when implementation begins. It is harder to include a dissenting community member at this point in the process since the decision has been made, and the resources have been committed. The leader's role is to help dissenting community members understand the history of the project and help them see how some of their concerns may have been addressed by others who participated in the decision making process. There is no reason to criticize community members for their concerns at this stage of the process. Leaders should think broadly about how to include the community members as well as how to include them earlier in the next issue that may impact them.

Community decision-making capability improves with each iteration of the process. Leaders will become more astute and know which community members will care about what, and community members will learn how to participate at a level that is meaningful for them.

Characteristics of a person in the Let's Go! stage:
- *happy and satisfied with the solution*
- *annoyed by latecomers to the community-decision process*
- *supportive of the implementation plan*

What a person needs to continue to support the process:
- *a clear timeline and process for implementation of the solution*
- *ongoing communication about the progress*
- *ability to offer input as the solution is implemented*

How the leader can help:
- *Ensure high-quality project management.*
- *Build in a community review process.*
- *Help community members understand how to engage in future community decisions.*

Notes

_____

_____

_____

_____

_____

_____

_____

_____

_____

_____

_____

_____

_____

_____

_____

_____

_____

_____

_____

_____

_____

_____

_____

_____

_____

_____

_____

_____

_____

_____

_____

Core Principles

Seven Core Principles
of Engagement

In our work with communities, we have found that successful decision making in controversial community situations requires seven core principles to be applied from initial planning to completion. In every poor decision process we review, we see at least one—and often many—of these principles missing. Conversely, when leaders are guided by all of the following core principles, positive processes and outcomes are achieved:

- *Include Diverse Perspectives*
- *Understand Each Other*
- *Use Experts Wisely*
- *Expect It to Be Messy*
- *Make Decisions on Shared Facts*
- *Take One Step at a Time*
- *Leave Tracks*

We encourage you to consider how well you are able to act according to these principles. Keep notes about which principles are most difficult for you to act on. These principles must be experienced in action by the community to make a difference in the community-decision process.

Include Diverse Perspectives

Each community decision affects distinct groups differently.

It is essential that all relevant interest groups or constituencies are engaged in the decision, especially those groups that may dissent.

Bring key advocates and dissenters together. Confirm that each

constituency has access to and agrees to the same set of facts and figures. Ensure that everyone understands the interests of others. Separate this step from solution generation.

Ask all to consider underrepresented viewpoints and whether enough of the community has experienced the Moment of *Oh!* Early and sustained conversations among advocates and dissenters are critical to effective solution implementation. While there is no "silver bullet" for successful community decision making, communities that do not pay attention to this principle are destined for failure.

Common Missteps:

- *Decide on the best solution before engaging affected parties, and tell people why the decision is the best solution* ex post facto.
- *When individuals challenge the decision, discredit them for lacking expertise, for not having all the information, and/or for their lack of participation in the announced public meeting.*
- *Tell them why their proposed alternative solutions are invalid or won't work.*

Key Considerations:

- *Have you identified the various interest groups?*
- *Have you invited representation from the interest groups?*
- *Do you have a plan to allow people to share diverse perspectives?*
- *Are you open to considering the opinions of others?*
- *Have you allocated enough time for the necessary dialogue?*

Understand Each Other

Understanding is the basis for a community moving forward together.

Decision making requires the community to expand its understanding of the problems, impacts, and various interests of the community. Communication, conversation, and relationships form the basis for this increased understanding.

Communication

How often have you heard someone say, "I communicated the message; I don't understand why they claim they didn't know?"

Communication is like the game of catch: someone has to send (throw) the message, and someone has to receive (catch) it. If the sender throws the message too fast or too slow, or if the receiver is not ready, communication will likely not occur. While communication planning often focuses on the sending of a message, it is only through verification that we can know with certainty that the communication was successful.

Effective communication requires three commitments from the sender:

1. Consider the message being sent.
2. Consider the audience receiving the message.
3. Determine how message verification will be achieved.

Just as the characteristics of the person catching the ball need to be considered in how you throw a ball (age, ability, and distance from the thrower), the characteristics of the message recipient must affect how a message is sent. When there are several different message recipients—each with his or her own priorities and interests—the only way a message can be successfully received is to employ different message strategies and mechanisms that target different individuals and groups.

Conversation

While sending e-mails, posting on websites, and making presentations may be effective ways to disseminate information, achieving increased understanding requires listeners to unpack some of what they think and repack their thinking with new information. The best way to foster this active listening is through small-group conversations.

When striving to help the community progress through the stages of engagement, small-group conversations are essential. Personal decisions require us to openly consider what we currently think with as much objectivity as we can muster. Respectful, quality conversations are essential for individuals to arrive at the Moment of *Oh!*

When asked what makes for a great conversation, people often cite respect, listening, safety, mutual caring, and interest in the topic.

When the community meets, these great conversation characteristics must be present.

Relationships

Quality conversations and effective communication depend on developing strong relationships across stakeholder groups. While we can define different stakeholder groups concerned about a specific situation, relationships are developed individual to individual.

The likelihood of complete agreement across constituencies is small; however, an atmosphere of understanding and respect founded on good relationships helps the community arrive at solutions that benefit the community as a whole.

Do not underestimate the time it takes to have quality conversations and build the strong relationships required for a community to make tough decisions.

Common Missteps:

- *overreliance on pushing information*
- *underemphasis on listening by leaders*
- *little effort placed on connecting individuals' interests to the situation/issue*

Key Considerations:

- *Do you have enough time to have conversations and build relationships?*
- *Do you encourage conversations among community members?*
- *Do you take the time to have one-on-one conversation?*

Use Experts Wisely

Expertise is very useful to civic conversations, but every expert also holds a particular point of view.

Most citizens understand that there is never one expert whom everyone recognizes as a credible source of information. Good community conversations are designed to illuminate the various perspectives on a particular topic. These can include views from people who have studied the topic more than others or who can convey a particular body of knowledge, but every person has a right to voice his or her point of view—however that point of view is informed. If all views are not heard and respected, a community has little chance of generating quality solutions.

Posing a few thoughtful questions easily demonstrates respect and civility. Leaders and participants may even discover new ways of looking at the issue.

Reliance solely on experts to frame a problem and create the solution leads to poor results for the community. Experts play a critical role in many community-decision processes, but their role should be limited to providing factual information and research upon which community members can base good decisions. The role of experts is not to *make* decisions but rather to *inform* those decisions. In the worst cases, experts impatiently and arrogantly dismiss concerns of community members, which is a breach of their responsibility as well as a frequent source of indignation and resistance within the community.

It is too easy to blame uninformed or uneducated citizens for sabotaging community decisions. Making the *right* decision does not necessarily equate to a *good* community decision. A community that doesn't support a solution—no matter how technically "correct"—risks frustration, broken relationships, and lawsuits. Leaders who place too much emphasis on their own or others' expertise can get locked in a battle to prove the "rightness" of the solution (often by bringing in more experts). The better response is to engage resistant community members in a review of the expert opinions, and take the time and effort required to address community members' concerns. This can sometimes be a slow process requiring strategic educational components such as community meetings, newspaper articles, surveys, and other mechanisms.

The good news is communities that commit to this process and dedicate time and resources to it will become better over time at gathering and sharing relevant information. The result is the community-education process becomes easier and easier. Community members learn where to go for information, and the leaders learn how to communicate with various constituents on future issues.

Common Missteps:

- *Rely solely on experts to frame a problem and to create the solution.*
- *Dismiss concerns of community members as uninformed or uneducated.*
- *Drive to the one and only "right" solution.*

Key Considerations:

- *Have you designed the process to encourage community learning from multiple expert opinions?*
- *Have you allowed community concerns to help frame the problem?*
- *Have you remained open to more than one "right way"?*

Expect It to Be Messy

Tough community decisions involve many opposing views, require time, and are—in a word—messy.

Since decision making is a human endeavor, and complex decisions involve many people with divergent interests, the process of getting to a community decision is messy.

The idea that a complex decision process can be laid out in a series of sequential steps is appealing, but it's more fantasy than fact. While we would like the decision process to look like sequential steps (A → B → C → D → solution), that is not how complex problems are solved.

To include diverse perspectives, the process must be inclusive and allow consideration of divergent ideas.

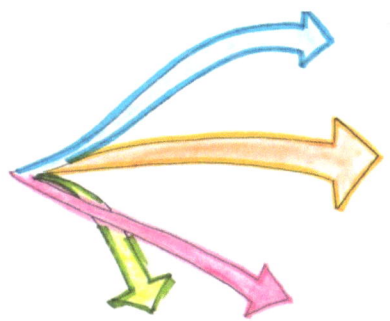

Only through divergence of ideas will the various constituency groups trust that they are heard and develop a better understanding of the other group's thoughts and interests. This trust and understanding is essential to achieving enduring decisions.

Leaders must allow the process to diverge in order for consensus to emerge. It is only after divergence that the community can converge to consensus. Timing by the leaders to shift the community from divergent thinking to convergent thinking is critical. Moving too soon will disenfranchise individuals who want to give additional input. Moving too late creates unnecessary frustration with the process. In our experience most leaders 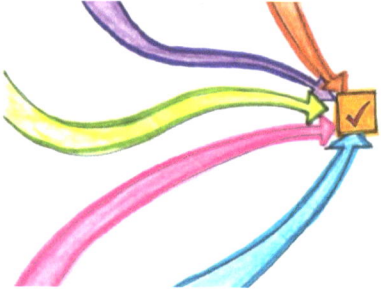 want to move too soon without realizing the negative effects of leaving community members behind. When leaders get the timing right, people are able to connect diverse perspectives and potential solutions in new ways to achieve a solution that supports the interests of the community as a whole.

Putting it all together:

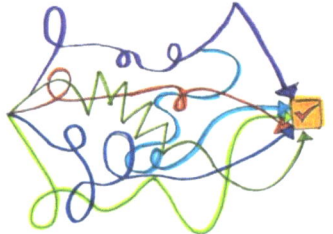 Divergence/convergence behavior can be seen over the entire decision-making process as well as at individual points and events within the decision-making process.

At times the leader and community members will feel like the whole process is coming apart. This is usually the time to press on and begin the process of convergence.

Common Missteps:
- *Avoid the messy, divergent process.*
- *Drive too fast toward convergence.*
- *Linger too long in the divergent mess.*

Key Considerations:
- *Have you readied yourself for the "messy middle" of the process?*
- *Have you warned others involved about how the process will unfold and that there will be some discomfort in the middle of the process?*

Make Decisions Based on Shared Facts

A foundation of shared and relevant facts leads to decisions that stand up in contentious situations.

The story goes that Henry Kissinger started complex, international negotiations with statements such as, "Today is Wednesday." All the people at the table would nod their heads, and the meeting would begin with everybody in agreement. The principle here is that we slowly build a foundation of facts and assumptions upon which everyone can agree. Sometimes the only clear agreement might be what day it is, but as the process continues, community members are able to find more and more relevant facts upon which they all agree.

 A community might base a decision on an indisputable fact such as "a flood destroyed parts of downtown" or an assumption such as "a vibrant downtown is important to the city's economy." Other community decisions might rely upon quantitative data related to the issue. A continuously updated list of common facts and assumptions becomes a critical tool for moving the process forward.

A critical role of community leaders is to communicate the shared facts and assumptions upon which decisions are being made. Relevance often becomes an issue because one person's concern is not necessarily that of another. It is seldom helpful to tell someone that his or her issue is not relevant. It is helpful to ask questions, provide information, and clarify intent so that individuals feel respected and understood.

Community decisions don't often end with 100 percent agreement. In the end a community will have some facts that state disagreement such as, "Fifty percent of the population believes fluoride is a harmless addition to the community water supply, 30 percent believes fluoride is a harmful addition to the water supply, and 20 percent does not have an opinion either way."

If the decision-making process is grounded in shared facts, then the decision process has a very good chance of moving forward.

Common Missteps:

- *Focus on differences and conflict first rather than common interests and assumptions.*
- *Assume agreements before agreements have been made.*
- *Forget about or submerge past agreements.*

Key Considerations:

- *Have you researched and anticipated points of common agreement for all interested parties?*
- *Have you built a regular process to review shared facts and assumptions?*
- *Have you built a regular process to acknowledge disputed facts?*

Take One Step at a Time

When planning, define an overall goal, define near-term details, and allow long-term schedule flexibility.

The more complex the issue, the harder it is to anticipate what the final solution will be. To keep the process moving forward, leaders must diligently plan for the next steps while leaving room for learning along the way.

The closer we are to something, the more details we can describe. In the picture to the left, it is easy to see grasses, rocks, and individual plants in the foreground. Farther in the distance, there are hills, and while we know there are individual plants and rocks in the distance, we cannot see or describe them. And there are many other things off in the distance that cannot be seen.

Both new problems and new opportunities will emerge with any complex issue. Communities must build enough flexibility into their plans to be able to respond to new information as it is discovered.

In addition people often think of public participation as a town-hall meeting. These are the big steps or milestones along the way. While major events are essential to the decision process, the little steps between events provide the greatest opportunity to move the decision process forward. Each interaction, casual conversation, e-mail, and phone call—as well as every communication, including articles, announcements, website visits, and surveys—is part of the process that keeps the situation in the public's eye.

Strategic one-on-one meetings and phone calls with interest-group leaders are essential to understanding and arriving at a decision that is widely supported by the community. The time between events provides an opportunity to reinforce what occurred in previous contacts and prepare for future interactions.

When designing a community-decision process, there must be a clear overall goal. The level of detail in the plan must be relative to how much is known and must provide for the interactions and activities beyond the major public events.

Common Missteps:
- *Create detailed plans for an unknown future.*
- *Treat midcourse corrections as a failure of planning.*

Key Considerations:
- *Have you defined an overall goal?*
- *Have you clarified the immediate next steps?*
- *Have you prepared yourself and others for mid-course corrections based on new discoveries?*

Leave Tracks

Providing a path for others to follow brings more people to the Moment of Oh!

We have already discussed the leader's responsibility to help community members through the stages of community decision making. Leaders often arrive at their Moment of *Oh!* long before many of the community members who will eventually care a great deal about the decision. Leaders will help the decision process tremendously if they are able to share the path they took to get to the Moment of *Oh!* and beyond. We call this *leaving tracks*, and we believe this powerful principle is too often neglected.

Imagine that you have several visitors coming from different locations. Each visitor will take a different route to get to your home. Some already know how to find you, and others will need detailed directions. If you live in a hard-to-find location, you would not assume that everyone could find his or her way without your guidance. You would provide detailed instructions that began from each person's unique starting location. Rather than focusing on where you live, you would focus on the path each person needed to follow to get to you. This same principle applies to providing guidance for people to find their way through the stages of engagement for community decisions.

The principle of leaving tracks applies not just to leaders but to everyone involved in the community decision. I might learn more from my neighbor who regularly attends public meetings than I would from a public official because my path to the

Moment of *Oh!* might be much closer to my neighbor's than to the official's. If my neighbor can walk me through his or her own changing attitude toward, understanding of, and commitment to the issue, then I can more easily follow his or her tracks to the Moment of *Oh!* and beyond.

At a community-wide level, a network of tracks is necessary to make it easier for others to join the community-decision process. The tracks for some will be different from those of others because different individuals and groups will have different reasons for caring about the decision, and they will have different ways of accessing information about the issue.

A practical example of leaving tracks might be a series of articles in the newspaper that tells a story from various constituents' points of view—what information was useful to them as they considered the issue and how their views evolved over time. Or a process might be designed that asks informed and involved people to hold neighborhood meetings to share their perspectives on the issue. A web page can offer tracks to accelerate engagement in an issue with a simple video to tell the story.

Common Missteps:

- *Forget how long it took you to understand the issue.*
- *Assume others' path to understanding will be exactly the same as yours.*
- *Fail to create processes for community members to follow others' paths to the Moment of Oh!*

Key Considerations:

- *Have you documented your own path to under-standing the issue?*
- *Have you documented others' paths to understand-ing the issue?*
- *Have you built a process to help community mem-bers find their paths to the Moment of Oh!?*

Notes

Applying the Core Principles

Core principles must be demonstrated in action. The questions below are intended to support the practical application of the core principles.

- *How will you identify the various interest groups?*
- *How will you invite representation of the interest groups?*
- *How will you allow people to share divergent perspectives?*
- *How open are you to considering the opinions of others?*
- *How will you allocate enough time for the necessary dialogue?*
- *How will you create time to have conversations and build relationships?*
- *How will you encourage conversations among community members?*
- *How will you take the time to have one-on-one conversations?*
- *How will you design the process to encourage community learning from multiple expert opinions?*
- *How will you allow community concerns to help frame the problem?*
- *How will you remain open to more than one "right way"?*
- *How will you ready yourself for the "messy middle" of the process?*
- *How will you warn others involved about how the process will unfold and that there will be some discomfort in the middle of the process?*

- *How will you research and anticipate points of common agreement for all interested parties?*
- *How will you build a regular process to review shared facts and assumptions?*
- *How will you build a regular process to acknowledge disputed facts?*
- *How will you define an overall goal?*
- *How will you continually clarify the immediate next steps?*
- *How will you prepare yourself and others for mid-course corrections based upon new discoveries?*
- *How will you document your own path to understanding the issue?*
- *How will you document others' paths to understanding the issue?*
- *How will you build a process to help community members find their appropriate paths to the Moment of Oh!?*

Conclusion

We hope you find this book valuable in your efforts to guide community decisions. Every situation is different and will require different emphasis on specific stages of engagement and specific core principles. If you would like to learn more about how we and others are applying lessons from *The Moment of* Oh!, we encourage you to join the conversation at http://www.civilsay.net, where we are building a repository of stories, case studies, and additional resources.

We applaud your efforts to bring community members together around tough issues. The process is not always easy (expect it to be messy!), but the long-term health of your community depends upon inclusive engagement of people on all sides of the issue. Our experience suggests that even the most contentious decisions can be resolved through the intentional application of the Five Stages of Engagement and Seven Core Principles. Please test them out, and let us know what works in your situation.

We believe an engaged society is crucial for a healthy democracy. Our organization, CivilSay, was founded to improve the quality of civic discourse one community at a time. We seek to change how communities approach tough decisions by helping leaders use these challenges as opportunities for their communities to become smarter and work better. Thank you for taking the time to learn our approach and for your dedicated service to your community.